AMERICA

Merry Christmas

A FRONT YARD VIEW OF THE HOLIDAYS

PHOTOGRAPHY AND TEXT BY

CHRISTINA PATOSKI

Merry Christmas America
A Front Yard View of the Holidays

Published by Thomasson-Grant, Inc.
Text and photographs © 1994 Christina Patoski.
All rights reserved.

Design and production by Lisa Lytton-Smith
Title calligraphy by David Kampa

Printed and bound in Hong Kong.

ISBN 1-56566-071-4

00 99 98 97 96 95 94 5 4 3 2 1

Inquiries should be directed to:
Thomasson-Grant, Inc.
One Morton Drive, Suite 500
Charlottesville, Virginia 22903-6806
(804) 977-1780

Library of Congress
Cataloging-in-Publication Data

Patoski, Christina.
    Merry Christmas, America : a front-yard view of the holiday /
Christina Patoski.
        p. cm.
    ISBN 1-56566-071-4
    1. Christmas decorations--United States--Pictorial works.
2. Christmas--United States--Pictorial works. I. Title.
GT4988.P37   1994
394.2'663--dc20   94-15297
                                            CIP

Cover
ATOMIC TREE • SANTA FE, NEW MEXICO

Page 1
POINSETTIA VIRGIN • FORT WORTH, TEXAS

Page 2
SNOW-BURIED LIGHTS • MINNEAPOLIS, MINNESOTA

Opposite
BLUE SKY, BLUE GROUND • SANTA FE, NEW MEXICO

Let your light so shine before men, that they may see your good works.

MATTHEW 5:16

HOLIDAY SPECTACULAR • CORPUS CHRISTI, TEXAS

*Stuffed animals ride on a mechanized seesaw, while Santa orbits the earth
on a rocket ship! Twenty electric motors salvaged from discarded cigarette and soda machines
drive the holiday vignettes in Billy Aldridge's lively display.*

O ONE CELEBRATES CHRISTMAS as enthusiastically as Americans, and nowhere is this more evident than in America's front yards. Galvanizing Old World traditions with New World vigor, they transform ordinary homes into personal wonderlands each December. While the Thanksgiving dinner dishes are still drying, millions of Americans start untangling and testing strings of twinkling lights, rigging them across the front yard shrubs and trees, and along the sidewalk, the garage, and even the family car. Life-size nativity scenes sprawl across the porch, reindeer prance on the roof, and busy elves hammer away in Santa's workshop. This spectacle is America's unique contribution to the winter holiday and is so thoroughly rooted in the culture that just about everyone participates in it. From lighted windows in New York tenements to lavish lawn displays on Florida's Gold Coast to glowing Madonnas in the border-town barrios of Texas, this American seasonal tradition shows no signs of waning.

This book is dedicated to the artists who emerge each December and make their yards holiday canvases. There are a lot of closet Rube Goldbergs out there, creative people who have no other outlet of expression. Some families decorate their yards as a form of neighborly good will, others take it on as competition or as a means of gaining celebrity. It is a hobby for some, a retirement project for others. Many people build their own special holiday installations; some even take over the garage during the off-season while the family car rusts in the driveway. Some displays are mounted year after year, becoming local tourist attractions. Others are fleeting, like shooting stars—up one year, and down the next—but new ones always spring up to replace them.

Christmas had long strayed from its Christian origins by the time it reached America, and was further transformed in 1879 when Thomas Edison invented the filament lamp. Americans soon began using small, colored lightbulbs to illuminate the Christmas evergreens inside their homes. In 1923, when President Coolidge flipped the switch on lights trimming the first National Christmas Tree on the South Lawn, the trend of decking the halls officially spilled out into the yards of America.

Suburban sprawl fueled by 1950s prosperity sparked an explosion of outdoor Christmas displays. Record numbers of people bought tract houses on the crabgrass frontier and demonstrated a contagious enthusiasm for investing time and money to adorn them for Christmas. Elaborate decorations mushroomed in front yards across the country, many growing more extravagant each year. One display sparked another, and soon entire neighborhoods were coordinating their decorations and even staging competitions. For many families, driving around the neighborhoods to look at the Christmas lights became a holiday tradition as sacred as *Silent Night* and Santa Claus. By the 1970s, the practice of outdoor decorating was so prevalent that President Nixon asked national television audiences to turn off their holiday lights in order to conserve the nation's dwindling energy supply. Plenty of people ignored him.

Today, local newspapers and television stations regularly feature the season's best decorations and in some cities, local bus and limousine companies offer tours of the most shining examples of holiday spirit. Bumper-to-bumper traffic attracted by highly publicized displays has, on more than one occasion, led to court battles between neighbors.

BLUE CURTAIN • LITTLE ROCK, ARKANSAS

*More than a dozen off-duty policemen direct as many as 20,000 cars a night that drive by
to see this Vegas-in-the-Ozarks showstopper. Over three million lights are strung five stories high and
stretch across more than six acres. Jennings Osborne employs a full-time, year-round
electrician to mastermind the wiring on this supernova.*

RED EXTRAVAGANZA · FORT WORTH, TEXAS
*Nellia Henry creates a blazing Yuletide glow by painting her terraced
brick-and-concrete front yard white, which acts as a reflector for the red lights.*

I began chronicling this American holiday custom in 1973. I had been intrigued for a number of years by an outdoor Christmas display in my hometown of Fort Worth, Texas. The owner's desire to outdo himself every year amazed me. A huge cross crowned the rooftop, lights carefully traced the television antenna against the night sky, more Wise Men were added to the already crowded manger scene, where a second baby Jesus rivaled an already existing one. Every year the display grew larger, until the overloaded electrical wiring set fire to the house and destroyed the decorations.

Over the past two decades, I have photographed Christmas displays in a wide range of locations across America—on back-country roads, in suburban subdivisions, in urban apartment villages, in trailer parks, and on palatial estates—concentrating exclusively on decorations in the front yards of private homes. Shooting with a 35-mm. Nikon camera mounted on a tripod, I made all of the photographs with extended time exposures, using only available light, with no filters, flash, or light meter. I shot in rain, in blinding snow-fall, always in the dark, and usually in the cold. I had four good hours a night to photo-graph, though I occasionally found the lights still burning well past midnight.

Initially, I sought out the famous and more ornate displays, but I became just as enamored of the modest ones, those that reflected the personal visions of the people who created them. I stopped at convenience stores and gas stations to ask for leads, friends gave me tips, and I collected newspaper clippings about noteworthy sites. I spent a lot of time studying maps and driving up and down unfamiliar streets, looking for the glow of lights. Getting lost was a nightly occurrence, but it frequently resulted in some of my most interesting discoveries.

Christmas yard decorating is a uniquely American folk art, drawing inspiration from diverse cultural elements, including Disneyland and the New Testament. The most compelling displays I have found are designed and mounted by untrained people who use nontraditional materials inventively and who are not motivated by profit. The holiday spirit filters through each artist's particular sensibility differently, sometimes in bizarre ways. Snow men join the Three Wise Men in nativity scenes, and reindeer fly over the crèche. People gift-wrap their window air conditioning units and improvise decorations out of everything from eggshell cartons to pantyhose racks to tin-can lids. The Virgin Mary meets Popeye, Buddha, the Venus de Milo, and Mitch Miller. Chimps ride a kangaroo. Reindeer are lassoed on a roof by a cowboy. From spare simplicity to outrageous excess, the ideas, skills, and budgets of these artists vary greatly, but the intrinsic appeal of their holiday spectacles is universal.

These photographs reveal a great deal more than the fact that Americans love to celebrate Christmas in their front yards. They are reflections of everyday life, pointing to uncharted avenues into the inner architecture of our culture and the private beliefs and attitudes of our neighbors. Christmas yard decorating is testimony to man's innate desire to create, to celebrate, and to share. I am awed by the zeal and diligence that go into making these personal beacons of light, and I come away from each Yuletide season with potent proof that the true spirit of Christmas is alive and well in the front yards of America.

Christina Patoski

PORKY & FRIENDS • FORT WORTH, TEXAS
Two well-worn pups and a bunny share the holiday footlights with Porky on this cheerful porch.
Behind them, a miniature Christmas tree sits perched atop the air-conditioning unit.

FLORIDA FANTASIA · HOLLYWOOD, FLORIDA

*Friends and neighbors donate hundreds of hours to help Bill and Alice Foster mount their
"Story of Christmas," which includes more than 250 figures and props and features a lighting system
that changes color every ten seconds. The Fosters give away color postcards of the display,
which also advertise the family's funeral home business.*

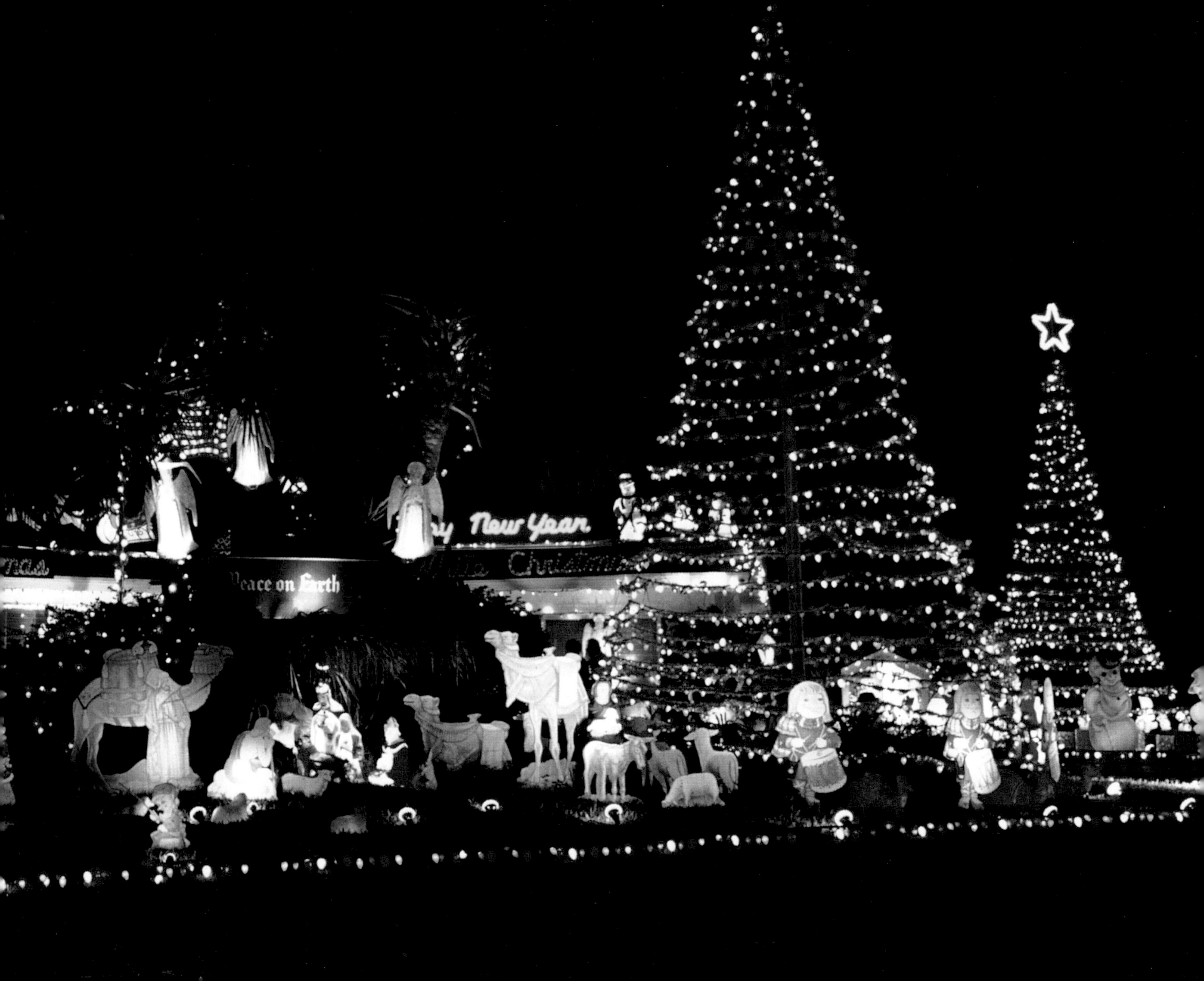
New Year
Peace on Earth

TREE ON HOUSE • DALLAS, TEXAS

Nat Baker sketched the outline of an evergreen tree onto a photograph of his house and then transposed it, full-scale, onto the façade. With the help of strategically placed screw-eye hooks, the single string of lights drapes to perfect effect.

HIGHLAND PARK LIVE OAK • DALLAS, TEXAS

The evening sky is illuminated by this giant oak laced with a profusion of colored lights.

RUSTIC PORCH • FORT WORTH, TEXAS
The custom of front-yard decorating has crossed over to other holidays.
San Juana and José Martinez and their three children decorate their front porch for
Easter and Halloween, but Christmas is their favorite holiday.

MINER'S CABIN • BLAINE COUNTY, IDAHO

This backwoods charmer burns brightly for the duration of the winter season.

FROZEN GLIDER · RACINE, WISCONSIN

Even in sub-zero temperatures, the Kleins' backyard glider looks inviting.

YELLOW YULE · BROWNSVILLE, TEXAS

*Enrique and Margarita Avila have opted for a sunny alternative
to the traditional red and green colors of Christmas.*

ELECTRIC CHAIR • AUSTIN, TEXAS

The chaise may be a better bet for relaxing in Jamie Lipman and Sharon Smith's
backyard, but their holiday throne of lights is a surefire attention-getter.

TROPICAL PALM · SAN ANTONIO, TEXAS

*Palm trees and tropical shrubbery are hardly in keeping with traditional
Christmas imagery, yet they offer the decorator some interesting possibilities.*

BIRTH OF VENUS · HOLLYWOOD, FLORIDA

Even Botticelli's goddess of love and beauty isn't overlooked during the Yuletide season.

VENUS DE DALLAS • DALLAS, TEXAS

*The Papathanasious celebrate their ethnic heritage by incorporating
the Venus de Milo into their holiday decorating scheme.*

BLUE MADONNA • FORT WORTH, TEXAS

*A constellation of white lights floats above a blue-lit Virgin Mary. The Holy Mother is venerated by
Roman Catholics, who have a number of Marian societies devoted to her, including the Society of Mary and
the Oblates of Mary Immaculate and in the Hispanic parishes, Las Guadalupanas.*

CRÈCHE IN A TUB • DALLAS, TEXAS

Joseph and the baby Jesus join the Blessed Mother for the Christmas season.
Most Virgin Mary yard shrines include an enclosure to shelter her; in this case,
an old bathtub provides sturdy protection from the elements.

VIRGIN ON THE PORCH • FORT WORTH, TEXAS

The Virgin of Guadelupe, the patron saint of Mexico, is always portrayed with clasped, praying hands, and wears a star-emblazoned robe surrounded by a luminous aura. A cherub always holds the Virgin on its shoulders. Cecelia Colchado has adorned her Virgin with a red veil, tinsel, and lights.

VIRGIN IN THE WINDOW • BROWNSVILLE, TEXAS

The Virgin of Guadelupe appeared to the peasant Juan Diego as a vision near Mexico City in 1531.
Today, millions of Mexicans return to the site, where there is now a church, to ask La Virgen for healing
miracles. Devotees in America also pay homage to the Virgin of Guadelupe every December 12,
which begins the three-week-long celebration of Christmas in Hispanic communities.

GERANIUM VIRGIN · SAN ANTONIO, TEXAS
Rudy Alemendarez's devotional shrine to his
Mexican Madonna proclaims,
"Although I am not here, I am your mother."

VIRGIN WITH HEADBAND · FORT WORTH, TEXAS
Climbing roses encircle the
Virgin Mary in Rosemary Lopez's garden.

VIRGIN IN THE DOGHOUSE • CHICAGO, ILLINOIS

31

ARCTIC NATIVITY · ST. PAUL, MINNESOTA

SHOWER CURTAIN NATIVITY · HALLSVILLE, TEXAS

ARMLESS NATIVITY · SAN ANTONIO, TEXAS

Purists believe that the baby Jesus should not be placed in the crèche display until midnight on Christmas Eve.

DWARFED CRÈCHE · FORT WORTH, TEXAS

Mixing the secular with the sacred can produce novel results.

NATIVITY WITH PEEPING YARD JOCKEY · **JAMAICA, NEW YORK**
*This fully loaded crèche scene sometimes overlaps into neighboring scenes,
making unlikely nativity attendees out of snowmen, soldiers, and Santa.
Finding the yard jockey in this photograph can be as hard as finding Waldo.*

LOUISIANA LIGHTS • METAIRIE, LOUISIANA

Popeye's Chicken founder Al Copeland found himself in court for three years when his neighbors demanded that he turn off the illuminated 18-foot snowman, the angels and reindeer, and the blaring Christmas carols because of the immobilizing traffic problems they were creating. The battle ended up in the Louisiana State Supreme Court, and because Copeland violated the court-ordered restrictions, his home, once an awe-inspiring landmark of 30,000 lights, now stands dark every December.

NIGHT IN TUNISIA • METAIRIE, LOUISIANA

BLUE-EYED BAMBI · METAIRIE, LOUISIANA

*This monumental 14-foot reindeer was farmed out to a neighbor when the courts
banned it from exhibition in Al Copeland's display.*

CHRISTMAS DOE · FORT WORTH, TEXAS

While reindeer have long been part of Christmas, Rudolph is a fairly new icon.
He was immortalized by Gene Autry, who recorded Johnny Marks's 1949 song,
"Rudolph, the Red-Nosed Reindeer," which was based on a promotional Christmas
story created by Robert L. May for Montgomery-Ward in 1939.

RUDOLPH • RACINE, WISCONSIN

GLOWING RUDOLPH • MILWAUKEE, WISCONSIN

HOLIDAY SKULL • ASPEN, COLORADO

A solitary buffalo skull is offset by a pair of folk-art Santa Clauses
and a wreath of barbed wire, at Janie Beggs' Red Mountain ranch.

SANTAS ON HORSEBACK · SAN ANTONIO, TEXAS

*Ed Clark is so crazy about Christmas that he never takes down his display and
keeps it lit throughout the year. He has slowly stocked his rambling spectacle by shopping
garage sales, flea markets, and discount houses.*

RIDING RUDOLPH • CORPUS CHRISTI, TEXAS

Two chimpanzees saddle up on a marsupial Rudolph mounted on a bobbing weight-reducing machine.

SING ALONG WITH MITCH • CORPUS CHRISTI, TEXAS
*TV repairman Billy Aldridge wired his daughter's cast-off doll to blink her eyes,
move her head, and play the piano, following the baton of Mitch Miller.
Small lights fill the mouths of the choir members and flicker to the rhythm of piped-in carols.*

CHOIR • DENVER, COLORADO

*Although Louis Johnson is totally blind, he takes great pleasure in mounting his
Christmas display, and relies on his wife to keep tabs on burnt-out bulbs.*

JESUS AND THE CHOIR • WICHITA FALLS, TEXAS

*L. T. Burns started out with a tree and a single blue lightbulb on his front porch in the 1920s
and added something new to his decorations every year. By the time he died in 1955, his "Fantasy of Lights"
had become a major tourist attraction and included more than 20 separate scenes, which have been
displayed on the campus of Midwestern State University since 1974.*

THE JOKER • LINCOLNWOOD, ILLINOIS

The Cascios have chosen a circus motif for their decorations, bringing the concrete porch lions into the act,
along with a seal that spins a ball on its nose. "You can't come up with a decorating scheme in one year," says
Dr. Samuel J. Cascio. "It takes several years of adding and subtracting and thinking about it."

JIGGS, BUDDHA, AND POPEYE · FORT WORTH, TEXAS

*A long-forgotten comic-strip character and a spinach-eating sailor-man
make for odd disciples to the sacred Eastern deity.*

TOY SOLDIERS · LINCOLNWOOD, ILLINOIS
*Representing each state of the union, 50 toy soldiers juxtaposed
with flag-waving elves line the curb in front of the Skul house.*

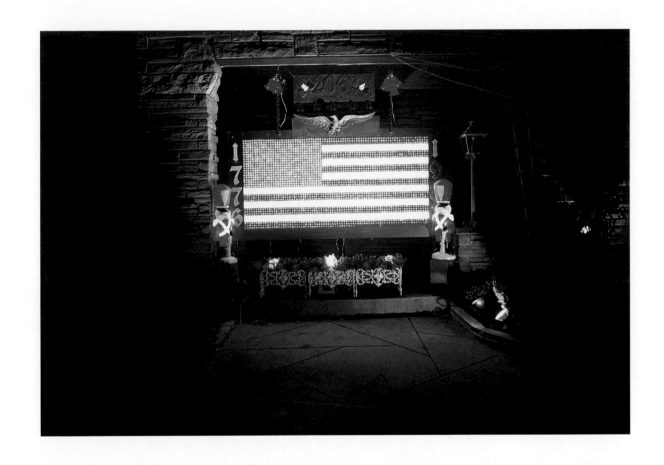

BICENTENNIAL PORCH • LINCOLNWOOD, ILLINOIS
*Dr. Vladimir Skul emigrated to America from Zagreb, Croatia in 1963, and designed the
first of his popular patriotic displays in 1979 to honor the American hostages in Iran. He built the
4' x 8' flag, which he also displays every 4th of July, out of 3,000 flashing lights.*

GOLD COAST BLITZ • HOLLYWOOD, FLORIDA

*Don Drybread started decorating in 1970 and expanded his display when his daughter bought
the house next door in 1985, the same year Good Housekeeping magazine voted him first runner-up for the best
Christmas decorations in America. But when the Interstate expansion cut into his street
parking spaces in 1989, he moved his private fantasyland to a nearby Indian reservation, where some
90,000 visitors per year pay an $8 admission fee to see his "Magical Village Holiday Theme Park."*

NATIVITY AND THE STAR OF DAVID • HOLLYWOOD, FLORIDA
All the bases are covered, with a culturally diverse rooftop choir hovering above
a classic nativity scene, and an affectionate nod of the yarmulke to Hanukkah.

YARMULKE BOY · HOLLYWOOD, FLORIDA
*Hanukkah, or Chanukah, is known as the Festival of Lights
and is celebrated for eight days each December.*

SIDEWALK ICICLE STICKS • FORT WORTH, TEXAS

INFERNO · FORT WORTH, TEXAS

Red light spills out onto Charles and Hope Medrano's driveway,
resembling a sinister Japanese sci-fi creature with glowing white eyes.

REINDEER STRAGGLER · FORT WORTH, TEXAS

HOLIDAY ARBOR • SILVER SPRING, MARYLAND

ANGEL ON THE FENCE · FORT WORTH, TEXAS

Following a stroke, John Lopez took up woodworking as a hobby
and now creates plywood holiday figures for his yard.

RAMPED PORCH WITH MATTRESS AND FAN · FORT WORTH, TEXAS

Ready and waiting for those last-minute holiday sleep-over guests.

TARA · FORT WORTH, TEXAS

*White lights transform James Riley's historic Texas home into
a fantasy landscape perfect for Scarlett and Rhett.*

LUMINOUS ANGEL • FORT WORTH, TEXAS

A trailing white veil draped over blinding white light makes for a powerful holiday image.

ASCENDING ANGELS • SAN ANTONIO, TEXAS

With a little string and stuffing, these white plastic garbage bags are headed straight to heaven.

BLUE CHRISTMAS • SANTA FE, NEW MEXICO

GABRIEL · ALEXANDRIA, VIRGINIA
Make a joyful noise!

NEW YORK NOCTURNE • NEW YORK, NEW YORK

HIGH RISE · BROOKLYN, NEW YORK

CHRISTMAS DISH • CHICAGO, ILLINOIS

HYBRID HOLIDAY · DENVER, COLORADO

*Tenants in the Windsor Garden Apartments put aside their differences for the
holidays to present a united front in the complex's annual decorating competition.*

CRÈCHE IN A TENT • SAN ANTONIO, TEXAS

The Christmas star leads the way to the Holy Family, who have settled in for the night by their pup tent.

SAN ANTONIO STAR • SAN ANTONIO, TEXAS

Scientists have many conflicting theories about the Star of Bethlehem,
hypothesizing that it was actually a comet, an exploding star, or a conjunction of planets.

VISION IN PINK AND GREEN • BRONX, NEW YORK

A blinding visual overload is produced by the glitter shellacked on almost every object in this display.
"Once a year we have this little splurge," say the Capolupos.
"This is our Christmas present to the neighborhood."

PARSONAGE · WASHINGTON, D.C.

*The Grace Royal Guards, a men's auxiliary of the United Church of Prayer for All People, design,
mount, and patrol the decorations on the home of Bishop S. C. Madison, who ministers to 130 churches in
23 states. Madison's photograph is mounted front-and-center above the door. The lights are on from
sunset to midnight, December 1 through January 5, and stay on all night on Christmas Eve.
The electric bill on this Capitol City dazzler runs close to $1,000 each December.*

HO, HO, HO! • **BROOKLYN, NEW YORK**

*The Comito family has been setting up their yard display continuously since 1961,
and still use some of the original decorations. A real-life Santa shows up on the Sunday before
Christmas to hand out candy to neighborhood children.*

SEASON'S GREETINGS · SAN ANTONIO, TEXAS

*Sgt. M. H. Macias' intricate Christmas display was legendary, and since his death,
his children have remounted it precisely as he did each year in tribute to him.*

SILVER BELLS · LITTLE ROCK, ARKANSAS
Jennings Osborne's neighbors have taken him to court for the 100 miles of lights on his property,
but so far he has followed the judge's orders to light the display for only fifteen nights during the season.
In 1991, his lights caused a power outage in the neighborhood.

Left
WISE MEN IN SILHOUETTE · LITTLE ROCK, ARKANSAS

SPINNING GLOBE • LITTLE ROCK, ARKANSAS
This mother lode of incandescence is the result of months of work by a crew of 40 electricians,
welders, and crane operators. "Moderation is not in my vocabulary," explains Osborne, who started
decorating in 1986 and soon found his 22,000-square-foot home lacking in space for his decorating ideas.
That's when he bought the houses on both sides of him.

Right
NEVER-NEVER LAND • LITTLE ROCK, ARKANSAS

FLYING OVER THE PALM · LOS ANGELES, CALIFORNIA

MELTDOWN · LOS ANGELES, CALIFORNIA
Step #1: Wrap the entire outer surface of your house in tinfoil.
Step #2: Crosshatch it with twinkling lights.
Step #3: Duck and cover!

RADIANT PORCH · FORT WORTH, TEXAS

TWINKLING TWILIGHT • DENVER, COLORADO

Outdoor plumbing aside, this modest home makes the most of a single string of lights.

COMPOSITION IN BLUE-GREY • SANTA FE, NEW MEXICO

FRENCH QUARTER DOOR • NEW ORLEANS, LOUISIANA

FIRE AND ICE • SANTA FE, NEW MEXICO
Luminarias are open bonfires that are lit to symbolically guide the Three Wise Men to Bethlehem.
The city of Santa Fe allows residents to burn luminarias on Christmas Eve.

ACEQUIA MADRE WALL • SANTA FE, NEW MEXICO
*The custom of lighting farolitos, literally "little lanterns"—candles in sand-filled paper bags—
is a New Mexican holiday tradition that has become popular throughout the United States.*

FLORIDA TRAILER • HOLLYWOOD, FLORIDA

ZEUS AND THE FLAMINGOES • HALLSVILLE, TEXAS

You can't miss the homemade signs pointing the way to David Romero's unique "Christmas Spectacular."
His homage to the season commands a 50-cent admission fee and includes a meandering tour
of his bonzai gardens, along with traditional and offbeat holiday tableaux.

WAYFARER'S HOLIDAY · FORT WORTH, TEXAS

Honk if you love Santa! Midge Lovell takes the holiday spirit with her
wherever she goes—cruising out on the open road, or just resting in the driveway.
St. Nick always leaves an extra battery under the tree.

TRICKED-OUT MUSTANG • AUSTIN, TEXAS

Robert T. Whyburn and Chris Wing's 1980 Mustang is breathtaking . . .
but will it make it to the grocery store?

TWO-WHEELED WONDER • AUSTIN, TEXAS

The motorcycle met its maker years ago, but Whyburn and Wing keep it decorated year-round.

RAMROD • FORT WORTH, TEXAS

All decked out and nowhere to go!

YULE TIDE • FORT LAUDERDALE, FLORIDA

Waterfront boat parades are popular maritime holiday events in the warmer climes.

CARPET OF SNOW • DALLAS, TEXAS

*Although we associate snow with the holidays, few parts of the country can actually
bank on a White Christmas. Walter and Bertha Ahlschlager have devised a clever substitute.*

SNOW FAMILY · MINNEAPOLIS, MINNESOTA

TUMBLEWEED SNOWMAN • FORT WORTH, TEXAS

ICICLE SNOWMAN • HALLSVILLE, TEXAS

COTTON BAG LADY • FARMERS BRANCH, TEXAS

GATE SNOWMAN • FORT WORTH, TEXAS   FROSTY • MILWAUKEE, WISCONSIN   ROBOT • WICHITA FALLS, TEXAS

ALPINE HOLIDAY · ASPEN, COLORADO

*This setting is so ideally holiday-like that Keith Leighton
can't help but leave his Christmas display burning well into April.*

BURNING BUSH • SANTA FE, NEW MEXICO

FLORIDA HOLIDAY • HOLLYWOOD, FLORIDA

SCROOGED · FORT WORTH, TEXAS

William Green is faced with a dilemma every Christmas, because he lives in a neighborhood
where decorating is practically mandatory, and he hates to decorate.

SANTA UNDER CRESCENT MOON • GRETNA, LOUISIANA
All is bright in the Gallicio's whimsical miniature village,
and the rooftop display provides a sumptuous sight to aerial traffic.

CORNUCOPIA • GRETNA, LOUISIANA

A bounty of toys and knickknacks, including Snoopy dogs, elves, Smurfs,
and Polaroid cameras, adorns the Gallicio's side yard.

MERRY MISCELLANY • NOCONA, TEXAS

Bill Richardson's place glows on the rural horizon like a football stadium.
Eleven 20-foot-high light poles tower above an eccentric layout of holiday scenes made from
discarded watch display cases and panty-hose racks.

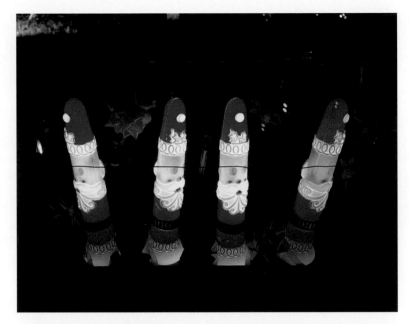

SANTA MISSILES • NOCONA, TEXAS

CHRISTMAS CANDELABRA • NOCONA, TEXAS

SANTA BEHIND BARS · FORT WORTH, TEXAS

Santa is doing time in the patio pokey.

SANTA FOR SALE • FORT WORTH, TEXAS
Cash and carry, 100 bucks.

ST. NICK AND THE BABY • DALLAS, TEXAS

*The original St. Nicholas was a kind-hearted bishop in Asia Minor who lived
during the fourth century and became the patron saint of fishermen and children.*

WAVING SANTA • ALEXANDRIA, VIRGINIA   SHOELESS SANTA • MILWAUKEE, WISCONSIN   BLACK SANTA • FORT WORTH, TEXAS

I could not have completed this Christmas odyssey without my guides, driving companions, friends, and family, especially my father, who provided me with loaded cameras at an early age and inspired me to dream, and my mother, who gave me the courage to pull it off. For keeping the car running and warm and for his unwavering support, I am eternally grateful to my loving husband. I am also deeply indebted to Margaret Patoski and Joe Nick Patoski for setting such high literary standards in the family.

To my distinguished associates at the Smithsonian's National Museum of American History, Eleanor Boyne, Shirley Cherkasky, and Lonn Taylor, my gratitude for the exhibition of these photographs. My appreciation to Lisa Lytton-Smith of Thomasson-Grant for tracking me down and bringing this book to life, and to Susie Shulman for helping me find the words. My thanks to Henry Allen for the wonderful opening biblical quote. To Vince Foster, a special gratitude for helping me with the first shot of this series.

For their inspiration, encouragement, and company, many thanks to Terry and Jo Harvey Allen, Janie Beggs, Tom Berthiaume, Katrinka Blickle, Julie Bozzi, David Byrne and Adelle Lutz, Camera Shop of Fort Worth, Jim and Susan Colegrove, Julie Corty, Kris Cummings, Gerard Daily, Jim Darilek, Devra Dedeaux, Georgeann Deen, Anne Edelstein, Vernon Fisher, Susan Freudenheim, Andra Georgas, Jim Gillespie, Ron Gleason, Will Golaboski, Marguerite Gordon, Susan Hall, Tom and Roberta Heinrich, Mary Hey, Dave Hickey, John Hughes, Tom Ingalls, Laura James, Charlotte Kennedy of Spectro Photo Labs, Michael Kornely, Bob Krueger, Cheryl Kurk, Mary Lattimore, Robin Laughlin, Sonny and Bert Lee, Billy Long, Erica Marcus, Kathy Marcus, Marilyn Maxwell, Elizabeth McBride, Sara McDaniel, Nancy McMillen, Marsha Melnick, Susan Meyer, Elsa Mitchell, Colleen Mohyde, John Morthland, Karen Murphy, Stuart Nielsen, Patricia Pape, Florence Patoski, Steve Proffitt, Judith Ragir, Kibbe Reilly, Joe Rhodes, Cynthia Rose, Julian Rothstein, Marnie Sandweiss, Robert Scudaleri, Tim Shepard, Robert and Amy Simon, Ric Spiegel, D. J. Stout, Clem and Laura Taylor, Joan Tewkesbury, Susanne Theis and the Orange Show, Kay Turner, Gary Watson, Peggy Weil, Mason Wiley, and Sharon Williams.

And finally, to all the people whose yards I have photographed: forgive me my trespasses.